Carmine Caruso

musical calisthenics for brass

ISBN 978-0-634-04641-4

7777 W. BLUEMOUND RD. P.O. BOX 13819 MILWAUKEE, WI 53213

Visit Hal Leonard Online at
www.halleonard.com

In Australia Contact:
Hal Leonard Australia Pty. Ltd.
22 Taunton Drive P.O. Box 5130
Cheltenham East, 3192 Victoria, Australia
Email: ausadmin@halleonard.com

CONTENTS

• •

• •

FOREWORD
· · · · · · · · · · · · · ·

"I might begin by emphasizing that there is no subjective judgment with these studies that is 'right' or 'wrong.' When you first begin playing an instrument, you may feel that you don't have a good sound. There may be occasions when a professional player or teacher may say 'that's a bad sound, therefore it's wrong.' But it's _not_ wrong; it's the only sound you have, and as you develop you'll have a basis for comparison.

Too much thinking about the quality of your performance—in the beginning—can only be destructive. Practice within the confines of your talent—and here the emphasis is on the word 'practice.' As you develop and play these exercises, you'll finally have a 'good' sound; until that happens, it's not the 'wrong' sound. Stumbling in the beginning is not unusual. We all know that a 'success' is often preceded by many 'failures,' so don't get discouraged. In the early stages, distorted notes may be all your muscles are capable of, and practice will improve them.

The body is always in a state of flux. Through the direct and repetitious activity of these exercises, you can teach your muscles that they can't remain in a state of flux. Your practice is set out to bring about a discipline, a coordination of mind and body. The results of this repetitious activity will begin to show gradually, in percentages.

I stress that playing a musical instrument is a muscular activity not unlike performing in a sports event. For a brass player, his horn is just a piece of plumbing; it's his muscles that do all the work. My method has often been called 'musical calisthenics,' which is appropriate because in order to play many instruments, most of the muscles in the body are working to produce a note. Nearly two hundred muscles come into play when a wind musician produces a sound. And it's the coordination of these muscles that I want to direct through this book.

Instead of thinking 'perfection,' encourage yourself to think in percentages, that is 'it's a percentage better than it was.' The words 'perfection,' 'wrong,' and 'good' should have gone out with the feudal lords: they have nothing to do with the art of teaching, and often their use can be a negative factor. If a teacher says something is wrong, the student has the right to ask, 'What's wrong about it?' Then the teacher will explain, and the student asks, 'Now, what do I do about it?' It is easy to dispense with all those steps if the teacher merely tells the student <u>what</u> to do. It's improvement, not perfection, that the student is trying to achieve.

Verbal negativity is not encouragement to the student. Teaching is giving with love, giving in a positive manner. This is such an important concept for teachers to remember. Unfortunately I have known many students who have lost interest in their musical careers because they didn't have a teacher who could communicate to them a love for the instrument and the art form. They may have been technical wizards, but those teachers could not translate the proper inspiration, and because of this they lost their students' interest.

It is my intent that this book will offer the musician the opportunity to improve his or her skills. I hope that you will find these studies beneficial in your musical endeavors.

Carmine Caruso

• • • • • • • • • • • • • •

This is NOT a music method.
● ●

This book is a clinical approach to learning to play your instrument. Its purpose is to cover all of the physical demands needed to play your instrument musically.

The book is clinical in that it shows you how to work your muscles so that you can use your instrument to make music, and to give consistency to your musical performances.

The clinical approach consists of:

      1. Sound

      2. Pitch (intonation)

      3. Range

      4. Endurance

      5. Flexibility

      6. Tonguing

      7. Technique

      8. Breathing

For the beginner it should be used as a supplementary method (calisthenics), while working out of any method book.

For the more advanced and/or the professional player, this can be used strictly for calisthenics. Follow instructions carefully.

●
●
●
●
●
●
●
●
●
●
●

• •

Interval Studies

The Four Rules

1. TAP YOUR FOOT. This is to establish the timing to which the muscles must move, so that they respond to the specific rhythm you make. (The tapping of the foot is the metronome for the muscular activity of the body.) For the beginning student who doesn't have a feel for meter, a metronome is suggested, with the speed set at ♩ = 60. Note: although the following exercises are comprised of whole notes and half notes, you may wish to change the count to fit your particular needs. Also, according to need, you may wish to <u>tongue</u> the first note and use a <u>breath attack</u> on the third note.

2. KEEP THE MOUTHPIECE IN CONTACT WITH THE LIPS THROUGH-OUT EACH STUDY. The mouthpiece must be in contact with the lips throughout the playing of each exercise until no notes are sounding and regardless of pressure or feel. The reason for this is simple: If you take the mouthpiece away from your lips, you'll have to regain contact and this will require two movements-one on and one off. Then every time you move the mouthpiece away, you have to reset the whole embouchure. The "whole" embouchure consists of five definite movements: 1) Putting the mouthpiece in contact with the lips. 2) Putting tension on the lips for the note to be played. 3) Positioning the jaw properly. 4) Angling the instrument properly. 5) The blow. If you leave the mouthpiece in place, you reduce the five movements to three, and if you leave the lip in tension you'll only have one movement—the blow. While breathing, maintain the same mouthpiece pressure and tension used for the previous notes. Do not be concerned with sound or pitch.

3. KEEP THE BLOW STEADY. The blow is both a muscular and physical function. You are blowing air through the lips and the steadier the blow, the more compact the motion of the air. The more compact it is, the easier it is for the lips to ride that airstream. As the airstream ride improves, the music will improve. For an analogy, think of the lips as skis on the water. As long as the boat is going, the skis stay on the water. When the boat slows down, the skis dig in. When the boat stops, you fall off. This is what happens with the lips when the air is not being pushed steadily through them. The activity of a constant stream of air "feeding" the lips will develop a better balance of the muscles.

4. BREATHE ONLY THROUGH THE NOSE. Breathing through the nose is done for the same reason as Rule No. 2: to reduce the amount of muscular activity it takes to produce a note. It's common for players to breathe as if they are sniffing, which will put air into the sinuses instead of the lungs. Breathing normally through the nose requires fewer muscles (fewer moving parts) than changing the muscular position of your lips in order to breathe through your mouth. This is a quicker way to develop an embouchure, because there are fewer variables to control, making it easier for the embouchure to find its place.

EXERCISE 1:

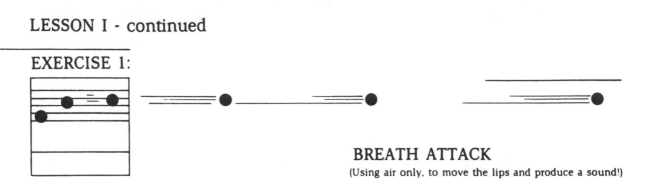

BREATH ATTACK
(Using air only, to move the lips and produce a sound!)

The Breath Attack is used in this initial exercise because it is the quickest way to get the lips in focus, to get them touching. Repetition of the Breath Attack eventually brings the lips into the best position. I call this balance; others may call it embouchure.

B = Breath Attack   T = Tongue

● REMEMBER: Start tapping your foot before you start playing to establish the timing and rhythm to which your muscles can move.

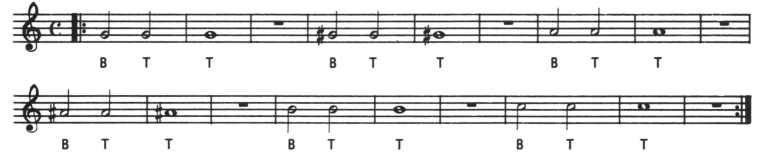

When you play these studies, treat them like calisthenics. Don't be concerned with how they sound and feel at this point, and don't worry about pitch or missed notes. The discipline to feel is physical, not musical.

EXERCISE 2:

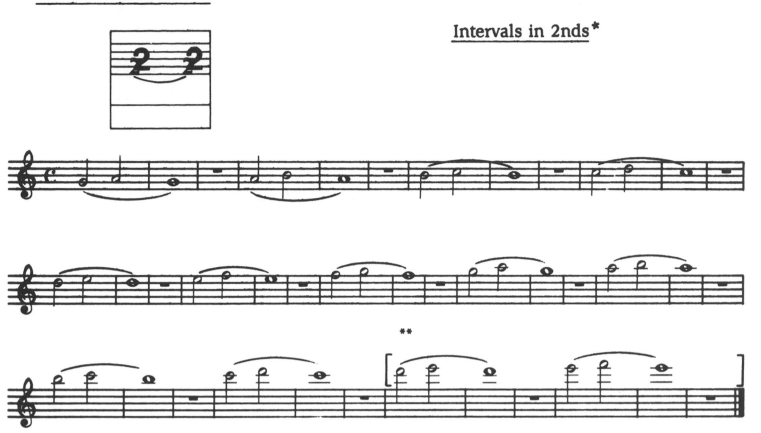

Intervals in 2nds*

* Be sure that you are slurring these intervals and not tonguing them.

** Play these notes only if you're able, don't force.

Again, when you are playing these exercises, don't be concerned with the sound, pitch or feel. Play with abandon!

Play as high as you can go until no sound comes out of the horn, but make sure that you complete the effort to play the particular interval. Take the horn away from your lips and rest ten or fifteen seconds. Then pick up where you left off and go higher, again until no sound comes out of the instrument. That is the end of this study. Stop for fifteen minutes or more and then repeat the study. PRACTICING IN THIS MANNER WILL INCREASE YOUR HIGH REGISTER.

During the rest period, if you wish to practice other exercises or music, feel free to do so. But do not use these physical techniques with other types of music.

If your lips become swollen, tired or stiff, wait longer before resuming the exercises. If they continue this way, then don't touch them until it is comfortable. Any discomfort will increase the chance of manipulating to reach a note and cause extraneous motion.

LESSON II

EXERCISE 3:

INTERVALS IN 3rds

(Intervals are to be slurred, not tongued.)

REMEMBER THE FOUR RULES: 1. TAP YOUR FOOT

2. KEEP THE MOUTHPIECE IN CONTACT

   WITH THE LIPS

3. KEEP THE BLOW STEADY

4. BREATHE THROUGH YOUR NOSE

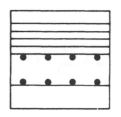

All of the following open sounds on each valve configuration of the instrument are called <u>the harmonics</u>, and, as such, are all the notes available to you on the instrument. They are important because you'll be working with every note as nature placed them on the instrument, not as valve configurations.

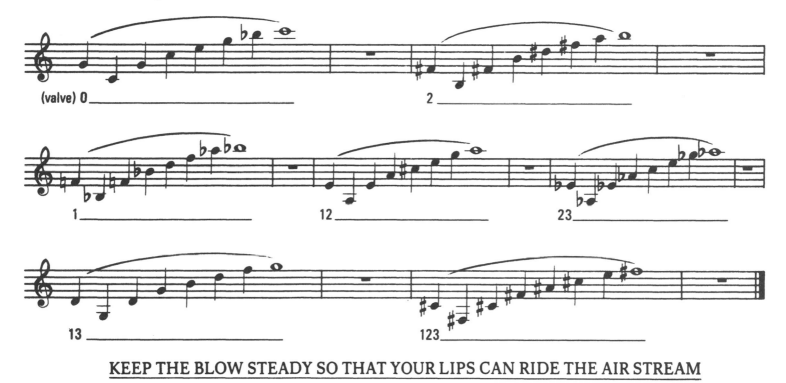

<u>KEEP THE BLOW STEADY SO THAT YOUR LIPS CAN RIDE THE AIR STREAM</u>

THERE ARE THREE PURPOSES FOR THE HARMONIC SERIES:

1. You are going from an upper sound to a lower sound without removing the mouthpiece from your lips. This is a subtle way to make you work your lips inside the mouthpiece without readjusting it. (RULE 2)

2. You are relating where you are coming from to where you are going.

3. Once you start the blow with the harmonic series, you have to keep the blow constant, even when no sound comes out of the horn. Continually doing so will eventually develop a better sound.

REMEMBER: BREATHE THROUGH YOUR NOSE!

LESSON III
EXERCISE 5:

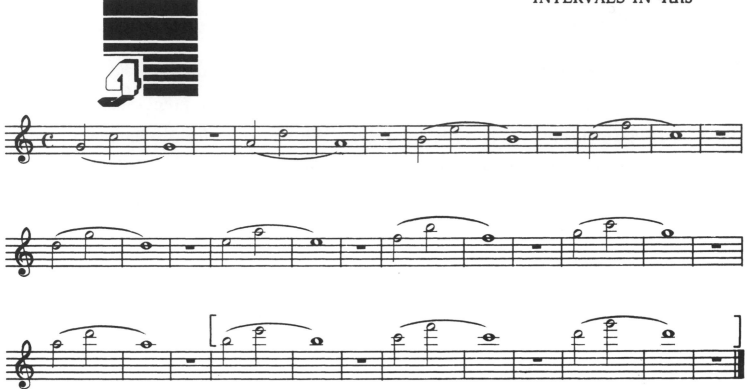

INTERVALS IN 4ths

REPEAT HARMONIC STUDIES!!

BREATH CONTROL — SOFT, LOUD, SOFT — STUDIES

The following are your first breath control studies. This exercise utilizes the same six "key" notes introduced in EXERCISE 1. These notes fall in the mid-range of most instruments and are therefore comfortable no matter what your ability.

BREATH CONTROL is the practice of blowing, which is the necessary demand of the instrument. These long tones allow you to concentrate on one movement, the blow, and will make it easier for the muscles to find their way into position. Remember to keep the mouthpiece in contact with the lips throughout the study.

To begin the exercise, blow a few "G's" (second line) to get the natural feel of "G." Then, leaving the mouthpiece in the same position, begin the study. Disregard the sound, pitch or feel. The distortion you may get is from overblowing, but don't be concerned.

EXERCISE 6:   Breath Control Studies

BREATH ATTACK/NO TONGUE

The speed of the air determines the volume. Increase the airspeed to play louder; decrease the airspeed to play softer. Count each set of three notes as twelve beats, subdividing by four. Increase the blow from 1–6; decrease the blow from 7–12.*

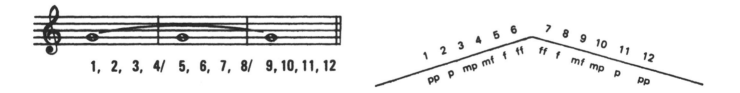

Tap your foot to establish a time for your muscles to respond to.
REMEMBER: This exercise is a physical action.

*Your sound may become raucous and brassy. This is a result of <u>over-blowing</u>, i.e. producing more power than the embouchure can handle. Through practice of the Breath Control Studies, you will develop a control of dynamics.

LESSON IV

EXERCISE 7:

ALS IN 5ths

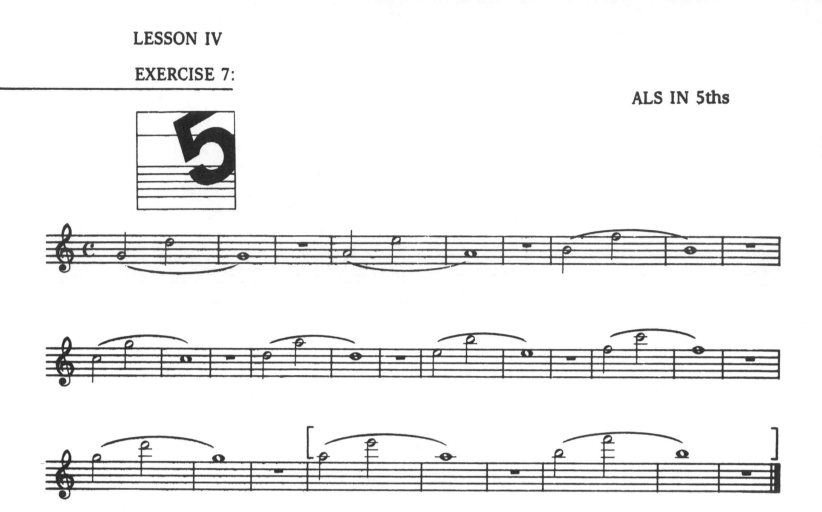

Play as high as you can go until no sound comes out of the horn, but be sure to complete the interval. Take the horn away and rest ten or fifteen seconds. Then pick up where you left off and go higher until no sound comes out of the instrument. Stop for fifteen minutes or more and then repeat the study. This will increase your high register.

REMEMBER THE FOUR RULES FOR INTERVAL STUDIES:

1. TAP YOUR FOOT

2. KEEP THE MOUTHPIECE IN CONTACT WITH THE LIPS THROUGHOUT EACH STUDY

3. KEEP THE BLOW STEADY

4. BREATHE ONLY THROUGH YOUR NOSE (If, at times, breathing through your nose is not possible due to a cold or allergy, then maintain the mouthpiece setting and breathe through the corners of your mouth. Do this only when absolutely necessary.)

Now, repeat the Harmonic Series (EXERCISE 4).

EXERCISE 8:

2nds IN THE 'BREATH CONTROL' — SOFT, LOUD, SOFT — SERIES

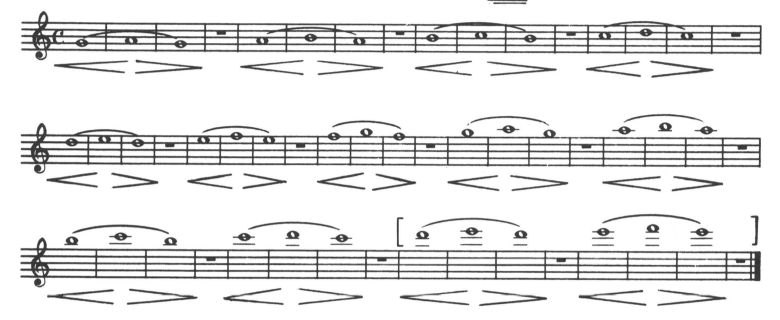

Once again, these seconds should be taken as high as possible. There may not be a marked change in your volume on the higher notes, but continue regardless of the sound. In time, controlled airspeed will develop on the higher notes and dynamic control will appear.

LESSON V

EXERCISE 9:

Maintain your mouthpiece pressure while inhaling through your nose.

EXERCISE 10:

3rds IN THE 'BREATH CONTROL' — SOFT, LOUD, SOFT — SERIES

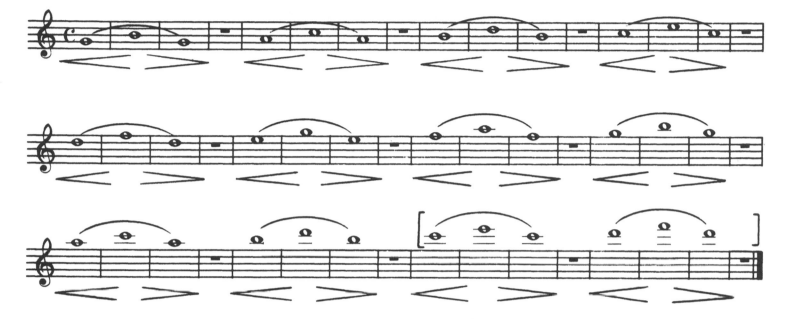

When playing your regular music, play as usual. Don't attempt to include these techniques in your everyday playing. With time, they'll be integrated into your playing automatically.

REMEMBER: <u>PLAYING AN INSTRUMENT IS AN ATHLETIC ENDEAVOR.</u> Timing, co-ordination, synchronization and balance are the secrets of the great athlete, as well as the great instrumentalist. The secret is to make the playing of the music look easy, but this can be accomplished only after many hours of hard work. Quite often, it is not the strongest athlete who wins the contest, but the athlete who can combine the elements listed above in the right percentages. The same is true for the musician; strong wind capacity doesn't guarantee a fine horn player, but it is extremely important when coupled with these other factors. <u>Timing</u> and <u>synchronization</u> are qualities that have to be refined in each musician's playing. In the beginning, the player has to be very aware of improving both these traits, so that later on he can "forget" about them, since they have become a part of his subconscious.

LESSON VI

EXERCISE 11:

INTERVALS IN MINOR 7ths

REMEMBER: Once you start blowing, finish the complete exercise with the same mouthpiece setting and disregard mistakes.

4ths IN THE 'BREATH CONTROL' — SOFT, LOUD, SOFT — SERIES

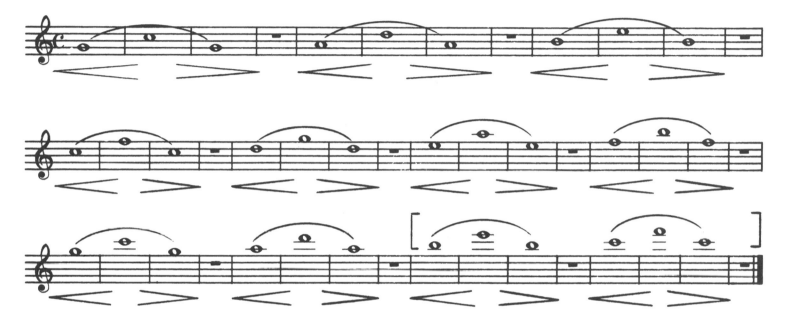

BREATH CONTROL WITH LOUD, SOFT, LOUD DYNAMICS

In contrast with the initial breath control exercises, the following will begin loud with full airspeed, diminish to soft by the sixth and seventh beats and then become loud again:

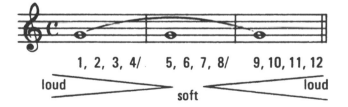

The initial blow of fast air will produce a loud sound. In the beginning, this sound may be raucous and unmusical due to overblowing, which is the result of extra power. In the past, the negative sound produced from overblowing may have stopped you from using the extra power. However, in this case, continue the exercise because it will expose the muscles to the type of conditioning needed to produce greater power (increased airspeed) and the resulting louder sound.

Begin this exercise by blowing a few "G's" (second line) to get the natural feel of the note. Then, leaving the mouthpiece in the same position, begin the exercise:

EXERCISE 13:

The first note of each group may be played with either a breath attack or tongued.

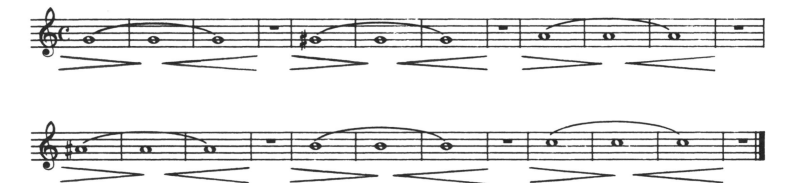

LESSON VII

EXERCISE 14:

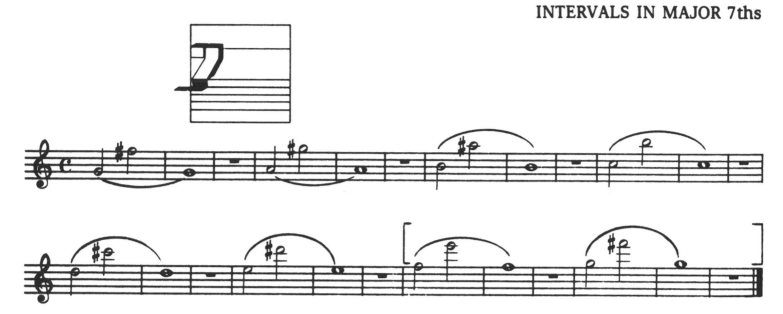

EXERCISE 15

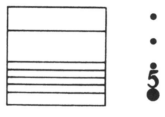

5ths IN THE 'BREATH CONTROL' — SOFT, LOUD, SOFT — SERIES

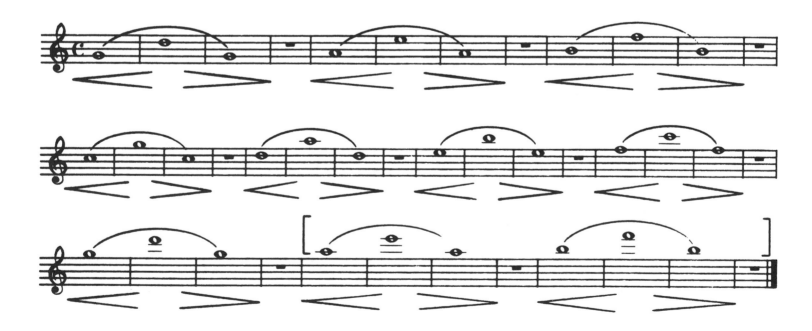

EXERCISE 16:

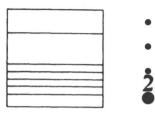

2nds IN THE 'BREATH CONTROL' — LOUD, SOFT, LOUD — SERIES

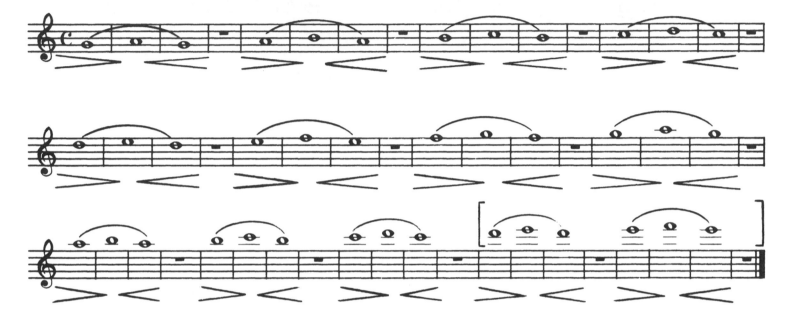

With your everyday music studies, play as usual. Don't try to make these clinical exercises part of your regular playing. Time and practice will change your playing habits.

LESSON VIII

EXERCISE 17:

OCTAVES

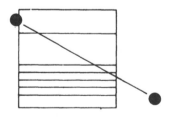

EXERCISE 18:

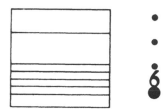

6ths IN THE 'BREATH CONTROL' — SOFT, LOUD, SOFT — SERIES

EXERCISE 19:

3rds IN THE 'BREATH CONTROL' — LOUD, SOFT, LOUD — SERIES

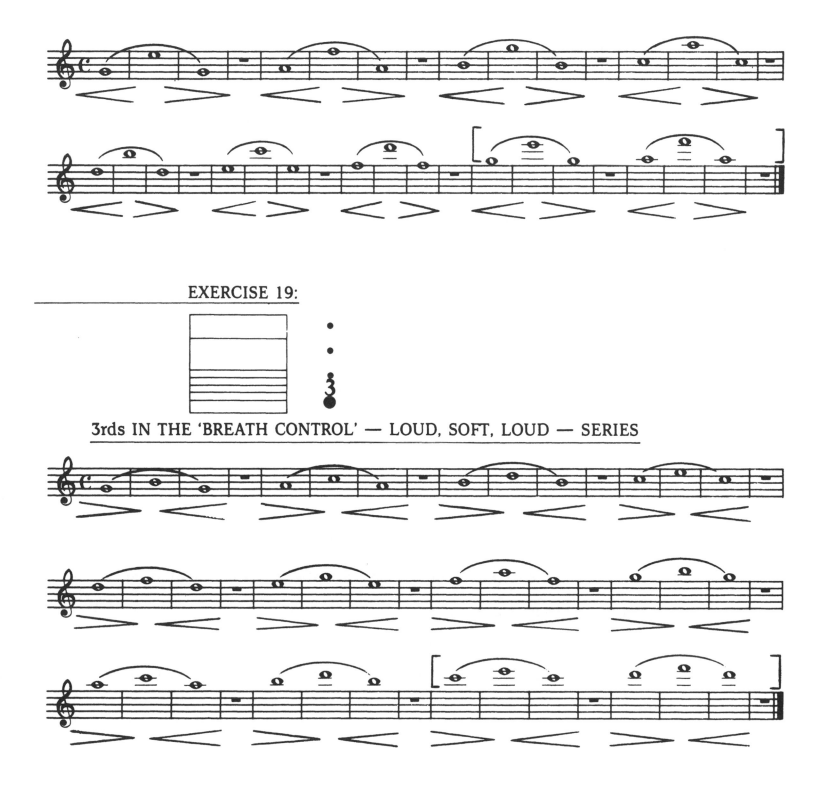

SYNCHRONIZATION / TIMING

It takes over 200 muscles to play a note. It's important to remember that before you can play music you must train your muscles to work together. The key factor here is timing: it will determine when the muscles start and stop a certain movement. The type of time is established by tapping the foot to a regular, recurring beat.

You expose the muscles to a physical activity by repetition to timing until the muscles synchronize into a conditioned reflex response. Once you develop a conditioned reflex with one type of timing, you can then extend the reflex to play longer phrases or subdivided ones.

For example: In the previous exercises, you've been subdividing groups of half notes and whole notes (long tones). No matter what the length of these notes, the important point-in regard to their timing-is when to get off one note and go on to the next note so that you land on that next note on time. In the beginning, it is always best to proceed at the steady pace of 60 beats per minute.

To subdivide your timing even further when playing whole or half note intervals, divide the last quarter beat into four 16ths before moving:

move

The action of all moving parts must take place after the fourth 16th note, just as in the previous exercises.

Don't be too concerned with the musical sound. The intent of this exercise is to strive for synchronization of muscular movement to a specific time demand.

REMEMBER: Proper timing is most important here. Better to keep the rhythm slow and the timing correct than to shoot for speed and neglect the perfect timing. Gymnasts and divers have an especially important guiding rule: if you can't do a specific move or dive flawlessly, don't do it. The same applies for music. If the proper timing sequence can't be achieved, slow it down until the right progress can be made.

LESSON IX

REVIEW ONE REGULAR INTERVAL STUDY EACH DAY

EXERCISE 20:

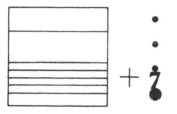

MINOR 7ths IN THE 'BREATH CONTROL' — SOFT, LOUD, SOFT — SERIES

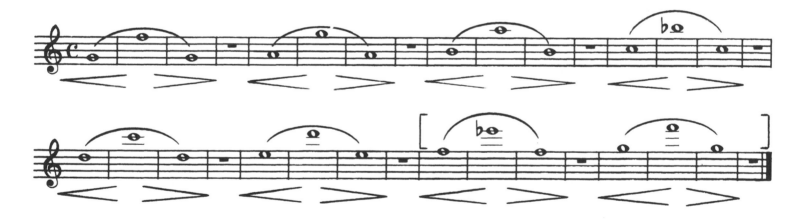

4ths IN THE 'BREATH CONTROL' - LOUD, SOFT, LOUD - SERIES

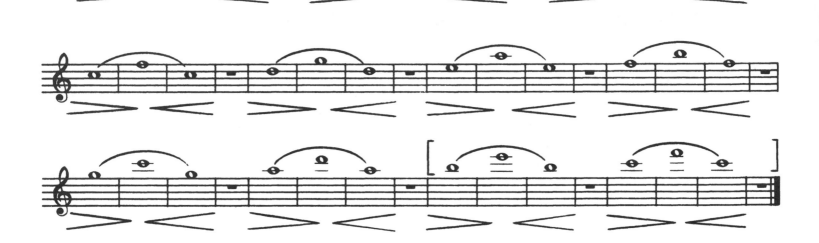

Remember to subdivide the last quarter beat into four 16ths before moving to the next note!

TONGUING:

Do the following tonguing exercise from G (second line) chromatically up to 'C' (third space). Take a breath whenever necessary.

When tonguing, use the syllable "TS" (instead of "TU, TOO, TA or DA") to prevent the chin from bouncing.

EXERCISE 22:

The order of importance in the physical activity of playing a musical instrument is: TIMING, BREATHING and then TONGUING.

A note is produced by the airstream exciting the lips. Consequently, the lips are both resistors and note makers. Pitches are changed by varying lip tension.

The tongue works on the airstream like a valve to interrupt that airstream. As a valve, it can only work on whatever airstream power that it is supposed to control.

There is no particular placement of the tongue that is most correct. The tongue will work anywhere in your mouth and follow the mouthpiece wherever it's placed. However, it is important that the lips remain constant in their motion, for if the lips are moving freely, then the air will move freely. With the power of the airstream constant, the tongue will work better.

When playing an instrument, the musician is dealing with numerous body motions. It's the synchronization of these motions that produces the desired results.

Synchronization requires perfect timing of all muscular movements. Therefore, timing is of the utmost importance.

LESSON X

REVIEW ONE REGULAR INTERVAL STUDY EACH DAY.

EXERCISE 23:

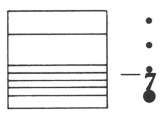

MAJOR 7ths IN THE 'BREATH CONTROL' — SOFT, LOUD, SOFT — SERIES

EXERCISE 24:

5ths IN THE 'BREATH CONTROL' — LOUD, SOFT, LOUD — SERIES

CONTINUE TONGUING EXERCISE (SEE EXERCISE 22).

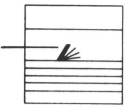

PEDALS

In the beginning, when you are practicing pedals, you may find that the notes don't respond with regular fingering. Try just lipping the notes by reducing the tension of the lips and keep the three valves depressed.

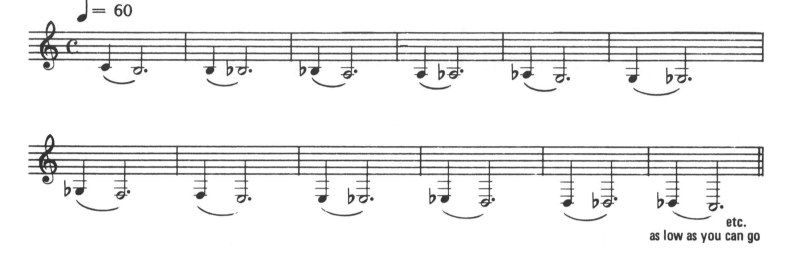

♩= 60

etc.
as low as you can go

It may take a while for the pedals to speak. But don't give up! Stay with them!

NOTE: After playing the pedals, <u>always</u> play this chromatic scale to re-establish the embouchure.

optional

The purpose of pedals is not only to increase range, but to release tension. The pedals do not allow the left hand to come into play. Consequently, there can't be any twisting or pressing. Automatically the lips become free—free to move, climb and sound. By playing the pedals and freeing the lips from the left arm, you will then release tension.

LESSON XI

REVIEW ONE DIFFERENT REGULAR INTERVAL STUDY EVERY DAY.

EXERCISE 26:

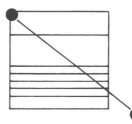

OCTAVES IN THE 'BREATH CONTROL' — SOFT, LOUD, SOFT — SERIES

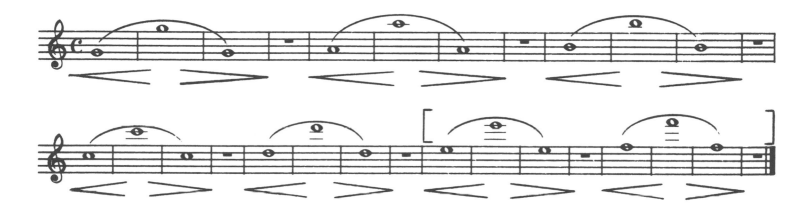

EXERCISE 27:

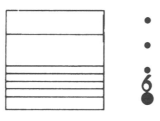

6ths IN THE 'BREATH CONTROL' — LOUD, SOFT, LOUD — SERIES

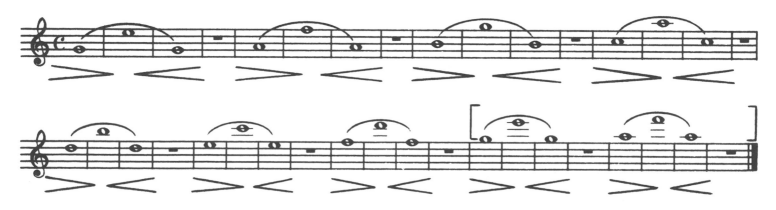

REPEAT PEDALS AND CHROMATIC SCALE IN LESSON 10.

REMEMBER: The lips are resistors to the airstream. The resistance intensifies to air, like water running through the nozzle of a garden hose.

LESSON XII

REVIEW ONE DIFFERENT REGULAR INTERVAL STUDY EVERY DAY

REVIEW ONE DIFFERENT 'BREATH CONTROL' STUDY EVERY DAY

EXERCISE 28:

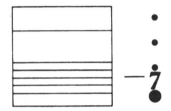

MINOR 7ths IN THE 'BREATH CONTROL' — LOUD, SOFT, LOUD — SERIES

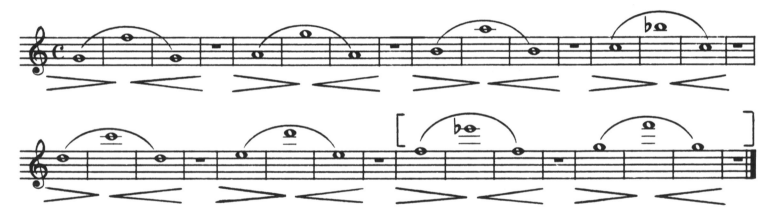

REPEAT PEDALS AND CHROMATIC SCALE IN LESSON 10.

EXERCISE 29:

CHROMATIC PEDALS (Based on Chords)

Slowly

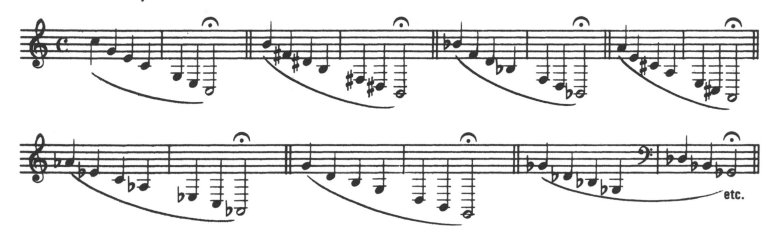

Play down as far as you can go. Follow the pedals with the chromatic scale in Lesson 10.

LESSON XIII

REVIEW ONE DIFFERENT REGULAR INTERVAL EVERY DAY

REVIEW ONE DIFFERENT 'BREATH CONTROL' STUDY EVERY DAY

EXERCISE 30:

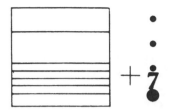

MAJOR 7ths IN THE 'BREATH CONTROL' - LOUD, SOFT, LOUD - SERIES

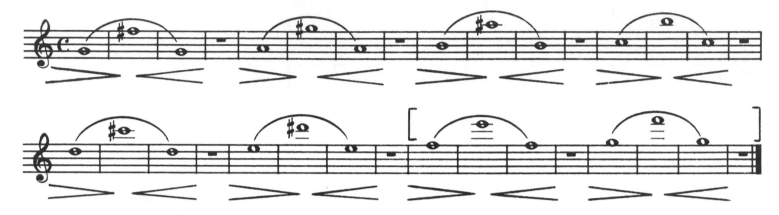

REPEAT CHROMATIC PEDALS AND THE CHROMATIC SCALE.

EXERCISE 31:

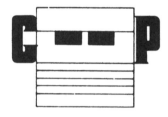

CHROMATIC PEDALS/EXTENDED I

Slowly

Follow these pedals with the chromatic scale.

DEVELOPED C SCALE

LESSON XIV

REVIEW ONE DIFFERENT REGULAR INTERVAL STUDY EVERY DAY

REVIEW ONE DIFFERENT 'BREATH CONTROL' STUDY EVERY DAY

EXERCISE 33

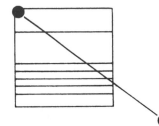

OCTAVES IN THE 'BREATH CONTROL' — LOUD, SOFT, LOUD — SERIES

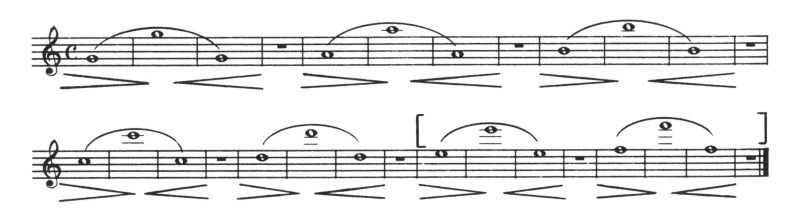

REPEAT CHROMATIC PEDALS AND CHROMATIC SCALE.

EXERCISE 34:

CHROMATIC CHORD PEDALS / EXTENDED II

　　　　Follow these with the chromatic scale.

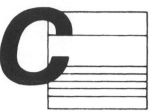

DEVELOPED C SCALE
In Triplets

LESSON XV
REVIEW PEDALS IN LESSON 10 AND CHROMATIC SCALE.

EXERCISE 36

CHROMATIC CHORD PEDALS / EXTENDED III

REVIEW CHART

REVIEW THE EXERCISES IN THIS RECOMMENDED ORDER:

1. 2nds Reg.	4ths LSL	6ths SLS
2. 4ths Reg	6ths LSL	2nds SLS
3. 6ths Reg	2nds LSL	4ths SLS
4. 3rds Reg	5ths LSL	Min7ths SLS
5. 5ths Reg	Min7ths LSL	3rds SLS
6. Min7ths Reg	3rds LSL	5ths SLS
7. ⎰Maj7ths Reg	⎰Maj7ths LSL	⎰Maj7ths SLS
⎱Octaves	⎱Octaves	⎱Octaves

ABBREVIATIONS

Reg = Regular

LSL = Loud, Soft, Loud

SLS = Soft, Loud, Soft

EXERCISE 37:

DEVELOPED 'C' SCALE

EXERCISE 39

EXERCISE 43

EXERCISE 47

EXERCISE 48

CODA

These studies are not flattering. Many times, they may not sound musically pleasant because they are calesthenic studies.

By this time, you will find much improvement in your playing when you're working with a band or orchestra.

These studies will continue to improve your playing as long as you continue to use them.

After the muscles learn to automatically respond . . . the <u>conditioned reflex</u> . . . that's the time to start thinking music.

It is <u>not</u> necessary to use all of these studies in the book at any one time. Use as many as will last about 20 to 40 minutes. This will give you ample time for your other practice.

You must do all of the studies in the book, however, whether it takes days, weeks or months.

Steady practice will create the discipline that allows you to do things the same way all of the time.

Good practicing, good playing and good luck!

—Carmine Caruso

HOW TO SOLVE
THE SEVEN COMMON PHYSICAL PROBLEMS!

1.	SLOW DOWN. If a particular passage of music is being played quickly with sixteenth notes and you're stumbling, it is wise to slow down. This is occurring because the muscles are not free, consequently not balanced, at the demanded tempo. It's recommended that you slow down to even half the original tempo to be within reach of muscular freedom. Working at a slower speed will give the muscles a chance to level out and balance. As you keep increasing the speed of the passage, you'll make it possible for the muscles to balance at a greater speed. KEEP THE BLOW STEADY. You can't run until you walk well. It is most important to build on these fundamental principles before tackling more difficult exercises. Speed doesn't come from practicing fast, it comes from getting the muscles balanced so they can move faster. Balance is achieved when all the muscles have the freedom to move.

2.	TENSION. Tension occurs mostly in the throat; this is where there's a backup and you feel a tightness. You'll feel as if you want to open up the throat, but it seems to be already open as far as it will go. This backup means that the muscles have become restricted and they are tightening up. When muscles are out of balance, it's normal for them to freeze and affect the airstream. Nervousness will often create this tension. If you always think of practice as the major factor for developing the muscles rather than being result-conscious, you will begin to eliminate the worry and nervousness about what's right, wrong, good or bad. Leave these thoughts behind and think of practice as conditioning. Your music will become a conditioned reflex and you will eliminate the tension. Remember: before a piece can sound good musically, it has to feel good physically.

3.　OVERBLOWING. When you surpass a certain loudness quotient on the horn, you may produce a note that's raucous, scratchy and generally unmusical. This is called an "overblow," and may occur when you begin the Breath Control Studies in Lesson 3. The overblow indicates that you have an overabundance of power and can't use it. This happens when you get past a certain speed of air and your muscles go out of balance. What you want to do is master the overblowing and turn it to your advantage; in other words, increase the span of your control over dynamics. By continually exposing your muscles to the greater airspeed—using the crescendo and decrescendo techniques in the Breath Control Studies—you will quickly extend the muscular control. The muscles will eventually stay in balance, even with the extra power you apply. The better balanced your muscles become, the stronger your blow will be.

4.　RANGE. In the Intervals Studies, it's suggested that you play as high as you can go until no note sounds. This is recommended, since the only way muscles will learn is by exposure. You'll hit those unmusical sounds, once again, but as you continuously play the intervals your muscles will begin to learn what is demanded from them in that specific area. A good example would be a dancer or gymnast, stretching leg muscles in order to do a splits. The muscles have to be trained and stretched slowly, in order to give them the new elasticity needed to perform the flexibility exercise.

5.　BALANCE. Is exposing the muscles to a specific physical activity until they synchronize. The better the muscles are balanced, the freer they are to move. In music, the freer the muscles are to move, the freer they are to sound. And, if they're free, they don't tire. For example, when an acrobat balances properly on his hands, he is less tired than if he is fighting to hold that balance.

6. WET LIPS vs. DRY LIPS. This has been a subject of discussion for many years. Most often, the player who depends on twisting or pivoting will want dry lips. With the pivot or the twist, the lips will slide off if they're not dry. There are a lot of wet lip players who play very comfortably. The bite inside the mouthpiece has a lot to do with the player who wants to play with dry lips, because that keeps the flesh inside the mouthpiece. Play the most comfortable way.

7. ATTACK. The beginning of a note is called the "attack." Many musicians delay an attack because of lack of feeling for the timing or because the transition from one note to another may not be smooth. The Interval Studies will assist in the transition problems. However, younger students should make believe they have a thread on their lip; spitting it out will assist them in assuming the proper attack position. You can't spit with your mouth open! Improved attack will come as a result of practice, as the player becomes more confident in his or her command of a musical piece.

In working with these seven elements, the main idea to remember is to always maintain a level of common sense. It is important to perform properly on a selection, so a player must surely find the right tempo for the exercise, then go about playing it more quickly until the correct meter is reached. TENSION and ATTACK are so dependent upon coordinated muscles, and arriving at this state takes time and concentration. No matter what the situation, we are always a little apprehensive going into it; as time goes by, we relax and feel much more comfortable with these new surroundings. RANGE and BALANCE are a refining of muscle response, turning whatever quantity of experience we have into a quality of experience. Musical activity should not be forced, but it should be a natural progression of each individual's talent and skill.

EDITORIAL NOTE

....

The actual technique involved in Carmine Caruso's teachings is only part of his great influence on musicians.

It is his attitude toward teaching that attracts more and more musicians in ever-growing numbers. Whether his students are schooled professionals or beginners, they are drawn to his teaching methods as much as to his musical exercises.

Caruso has spent many years formulating his concepts and he speaks with the confidence only successful results can generate.

THE GREAT CARUSO

Few men become idols while they live. One who has, is Carmine Caruso.

The name Carmine Caruso is well-known in many parts of the world. Brass players from Europe, Canada, Mexico and South America have left their homes to come to New York to study with him. He has a reputation for being able to help improve players just starting out, detoured talents, and players who already perform well. A list of his students reads like a Who's Who. Some of them refer to Carmine as the patron-saint of brass players.

What went into the making of this great and famous teacher? An extensive knowledge of music, a considerate attitude toward students, coupled with the ability to teach, and a question asked by chance.

When Carmine was three years old his father, Paul Caruso, began to teach him to play the piano. At four, it was discovered that he could remember tones—the feat musicians refer to as absolute pitch. The boy was a prodigy with a promising career as a pianist.

But at the age of eight Carmine gave up the piano. He had fallen madly in love with the violin. His teacher, now, was another member of his family, his older brother, Jimmy, whom Carmine adored. The violin became an obsession. Carmine would practice before school; he would practice when he came home from school for lunch; he would practice as soon as he came home from school in the afternoon. The last thing he would do before going to bed at night was to lay his beloved violin on the chair beside his bed.

When Carmine was seventeen, the saxophone was the rage. He wanted badly to play one. After all, his father was now playing one. But, alas, for some reason, it was his father who did not want him to play the saxophone. He forbade him to do so, in fact. But young Caruso was not to be denied. Despite his father's wishes, Carmine found his own teacher and an instrument to practice on.

Who was the teacher? His own father! Carmine would watch his father play, match up the fingerings with the sounds he heard (don't forget, he had perfect pitch) and remember them.

Where did he get an instrument to practice on? Again, his father. Carmine would play his father's horn whenever his father went out. His father never caught him because Carmine's mother would keep watch, looking out the window to warn of the elder Caruso's return.

Three months after starting on the saxophone, Carmine was playing sax in several bands.

Most of his playing career he made his living as a saxophone player in ballrooms and on radio shows. Vincent Lopez, Emil Coleman, Lester Lanin, and Meyer Davis were some of the leaders he worked for. The last big band he played with was Russ Morgan's.

In 1941 Carmine gave up the big bands in favor of a career of full-time teaching and freelance playing.

To his East Harlem home at 241 East 112th Street, students came to study saxophone, clarinet, flute and violin. He continued to teach at home until 1957, when his house was torn down to make way for a housing project.

One of his students was Nick Riviello, a saxophone player with Vincent Lopez. Riviello had been studying with Carmine for many years. Nick was sold on Carmine but it took him three and a half years to convince another saxophone player in the Lopez band, Armand Camgros, that Carmine could help him. After Camgros began to study with Carmine, he too became a believer. One day Camgros asked whether or not the principles that Carmine had taught him were applicable to brass players. Carmine said that they were.

In 1942 Camgros sent Carmine his first trumpet student, Lou Oles. Oles was also a member of the Vincent Lopez band.

Within a year after taking on Lou Oles, Carmine had forty brass students. The legend had begun.

Now began a parade of brass cripples, beginners, and the good players who became better. Carmine discovered that he had the ability to reach and help many brass players at all stages of development.

Of the cripples, he remembers vividly the one he refers to as "my basket case."

This was a player who had been much in demand in the business. A man with a reputation and the talent to match it. But this gifted performer had overworked his chops to the point that he could get no sound out of his trumpet. Though doubtful of Carmine's ability to help him, Carmine was his last hope. For the year and a half that it took Carmine to bring him around, this man earned his living driving a school bus.

Ray Copeland is grateful to Carmine Caruso for restoring him to the joy of making his living at something he likes to do.

Says Ray, "Carmine is a master psychologist and half of my problem was psychological."

"I had built up reasons in my mind why I couldn't play. I used to go to Carmine tensed up and over-anxious. Carmine wouldn't let me play right away. We would talk for forty-five minutes or so and by then Carmine would have psyched me into playing things I didn't think I could play."

"Psychology is half the battle of playing the trumpet. Everything has to be positive."

Ray's remarks point up some of Carmine's attitudes toward teaching. Carmine says, "Teaching should not be a whipping of the student with his inadequacies. The student should play with love, not fear."

He does not use the word 'mistake' when talking to students. What others call mistakes, Caruso says, "are due to carelessness, the inability of the player, or both." Instead of telling the student that his execution is wrong or bad, Carmine tells him what to do.

He sums up his teaching philosophy this way, "Teaching should be done with love. It's a giving."

Small wonder then that Carmine is revered by his students. He has helped them improve their playing. But also, they know that he loves them.

They respect the teacher, but they admire and love the man.

Walk down the street with Carmine and you can spot his friends and students by the approaching smiles.

—Bill Harrison

NO PIGEONS FOR CARMINE — ONLY LOVE
by Dr. Charles Colin

You may someday have an opportunity to become awestricken with the hustle-bustle of New York City, the BIG APPLE. Imagine yourself in glittering Times Square. Your eyes are drawn to the statue of George M. Cohan, yesteryear's immortal impresario. Countless pigeons hover about the monument that overlooks the Big White Way, but Cohan stands proud, Broadway's lord and master.

Approximately 50 yards from this historic spot, just off Broadway on West 46th Street, a sensitive ear stops and inquires about a series of sporadic, stop-and-go brass sounds. Curiosity lures you to the source of these unending short exercises in intervals which build higher and higher until they sky-rocket. Now you're on edge. How high can a brass instrument climb? Is there no ceiling? Real brasspersons have an innate lust to learn the answer.

You follow the sounds to a large, ordinary, unimpressive building. Still curious, you wander through the miniature entrance, searching for the source of those haunting simple long tones, or slower-than-slow drawn out intervals. The bulletin board holds no clue to any musical enterprises.

Just when you're ready to give up on joining a universal Brass Family—a lady steps out of the elevator, senses your confusion and unravels the mystery.

"Oh, those sounds. That's Caruso. Take the elevator to the fifth floor."

You ascend with renewed confidence and even more curiosity. Again, no signs on the doors of the fifth floor, but those mystifying sounds draw you to a door at the end of a dim corridor. On the door, the name "Jimmy Caruso" is simply printed on a small card.

What do you have to lose; you've come this far? Just knock on the door and see what happens. Curiosity has the better of you.

As soon as you knock, the door opens and there before you is a white-bearded man, short in stature, with smiling eyes, in a white sweatshirt and oversized earphones perched on his head. A gracious man, he radiates a warm fatherly welcome, and extends a heartfelt handshake that makes you feel you have known him all your life.

You explain that you are a trumpet player from out of town and, utterly entranced, you followed the magical sounds.

"Great! Welcome! Have a seat.I'm giving a lesson and you are more than welcome to watch what's happening with the students who are waiting," is the surprising invitation.

In your bewilderment you try to put all the pieces together. No name on the door downstairs, no sign anywhere, the fantasy grows as you become aware of an aura of unassuming simplicity. Plain and unadorned, the room consists of a few well-worn chairs, small scatter rugs and bookcases.

Is this the Carmine Caruso whose legendary reputation has spread around the world? The man with a following of brass students who have worshipped him for over fifty years and pray for his daily happiness and health?

Another awe-inspiring incident occurs. A famous Hollywood record producer and trumpet celebrity phones from California for his weekly trumpet lesson. When Carmine completes the hour-long lesson, he casually mentions to his receptive audience that the phone call was from Herb Alpert.

Who would believe that following the lure of a few strange sounds could change the course of a musician's life? Yet, this is a miracle that occurs regularly through the genius of Carmine Caruso. I have witnessed it, time and again. If it is ever within my power, there will be another statue right smack in the center of Times Square. Why? Because Carmine Caruso has proven himself to be one of the Brass Family's great heroes.

Whether or not the statue becomes a reality, there will not be just pigeons that pay daily homage. There will be a more meaningful and everlasting tribute to a humble man whose creed in life has been "to do good." He lovingly adopts all his students with fatherly warmth. There will be his students and the students of his students to honor Carmine Caruso, a humble and simple man with the genius to teach and with the naturalness of childlike love for his fellow people.